One of the nicest things in my life
is my friendship with you
and even if we don't have a lot of time
to spend with each other
I want you to always know
how much I appreciate you
and our friendship

— Susan Polis Schutz

Other books in this series...

Blue Mountain Arts®

A Mother Is Love

I Love You Soooo Much
by Douglas Pagels

I'd Love to Give These Gifts to You

Keep Believing in Yourself and Your Special Dreams

Sister, You Have a Special Place in My Heart

The Greatest Gift of All Is... A Daughter like You

The Greatest Gift of All Is... A Son like You

A Friend
Lives in Your Heart
Forever

A Collection of
the Thoughts and Feelings
All Friends Want to Share

SPS Studios™
Boulder, Colorado

Library of Congress Catalog Card Number: 2001005343
ISBN: 0-88396-609-3

We wish to thank Susan Polis Schutz for permission to reprint the following poems that appear in this publication: "Knowing that you are always here to understand..." and "There is no need for an outpouring of words...." Copyright © 1972, 1974 by Continental Publications. And for "A Friend Is Someone Special," "Thank You for Being My Friend," "You Are a Perfect Friend," "Our Friendship," "Some people will be your friend...," and "Friends Are Forever." Copyright © 1982, 1983, 1984, 1986, 1996 by Stephen Schutz and Susan Polis Schutz. All rights reserved.

ACKNOWLEDGMENTS appear on page 48.

Certain trademarks are used under license.

Manufactured in Thailand
First Printing: January 2002

♲ This book is printed on recycled paper.

Library of Congress Cataloging - in - Publication Data

A friend lives in your heart forever : a collection of the thoughts and feelings all friends want to share.
        p. cm.
    ISBN 0-88396-609-3 (hardcover : alk. paper)
    1. Friendship—Poetry.   2. American poetry.   I. SPS Studios.
    PS595.F74 F75 2001
      811.008'0353—dc21

                                                                          2001005343
                                                                              CIP

SPS Studios, Inc.
P.O. Box 4549, Boulder, Colorado 80306

Contents
(Authors listed in order of first appearance)

Susan Polis Schutz

Sydney Nealson

Donna Fargo

Collin McCarty

Laurel Atherton

Barbara J. Hall

Ashley Rice

L. N. Mallory

Barbara Cage

R. L. Keith

Laura V. Nicholson

Vickie M. Worsham

Vincent Arcoleo

M. Maxine Largman

A. Rogers

Kathleen L. Biela

Jennifer Kristin Ellis

Cammie Charles

Jane Wright Roberts

Acknowledgments

Friends Are Forever

Friends always remember so well
all the things they did together
all the subjects they discussed
all the mistakes they made
all the fun they had

Friends always remember
how their friendship
was such a stabilizing force
during confusing times
in their lives

Friends may have different lifestyles
live in different places
and interact with different people
but no matter how much
their lives may change
their friendship remains the same

I know that throughout my life
wherever I am
I will always
remember so well
and cherish our friendship
as one of the best
I have ever known

— Susan Polis Schutz

You Are a Very Special Person

I want you to know how amazing you are.
I want you to know how much you're
treasured and celebrated and quietly thanked.

I want you to feel really good...
   about who you are.
About all the great things you do!
I want you to appreciate your uniqueness.
Acknowledge your talents and abilities.
Realize what a beautiful soul you have.
Understand the wonder within.

You make so much sun shine through, and you inspire so much joy in the lives of everyone who is lucky enough to know you.

You are a very special person, giving so many people a reason to smile. You deserve to receive the best in return, and one of my heart's favorite hopes is that the happiness you give away will come back to warm you each and every day of your life.

— Sydney Nealson

Friends

They're like flowers in the gardens of our lives.
They're the permanent occupants in the rooms
   of our hearts.
They're in our thought spaces; they're our
   support system, without which we'd be lost.
They balance our small world and make it
   turn, turn, turn.

Friends harmonize with us on the songs
   we love to sing.
They give us hope and help us to stay strong.
They are the ones we call when we're
   lonesome and need someone on our side
To give us an encouraging word, a helpful
   hand, a place to be ourselves.

Friends care when others don't know how to.
They help us when we need it most.
They are like our very own guardian angels.
They make us feel that we're not alone.

Thanks for being the kind of friend I need.

— Donna Fargo

Some people will be your friend
because of whom you know
Some people will be your friend
because of your position
Some people will be your friend
because of the way you look
Some people will be your friend
because of your possessions
But the only real friends
are the people who will be your friends
because they like you for how you are inside
Thank you for being
one of the very few people in my life
who is a real friend

— Susan Polis Schutz

Promise Me This

Promise me you'll always remember what a special person you are ❧ Promise me you'll hold on to your hopes and reach out for your stars ❧ Promise me you'll live with happiness over the years and over the miles ❧ Promise me that when you think of me, it will always be with a smile ❧ Promise me you'll "remember when..." and you'll always "look forward to..." ❧ Promise me you'll do the things you have always wanted to do ❧ Promise me you'll cherish your dreams as treasures you have kept ❧ Promise me you'll enjoy life day by day and step by step ❧ Promise me you'll always remember the wishes I have for you...

For I wish you a life of love and joy
and all your dreams come true.

— Collin McCarty

Because You Are My Friend...

Because you are my friend, I know that I can always turn to you. Every time I do, I know that I can find the reflection of one of the world's most wonderful smiles on your face... and I know that it will always inspire a smile inside me.

Thank you for being all that you are. I have learned so much... about you, about life, about talking things over and opening up... in the time I have known you. I have been given the sweet and precious knowledge that can only come from understanding what it means to be a friend.

Within that wonderful place where the two circles of our lives overlap... is where I am happiest. It's where everything is always all right. I'm safe and secure there. It's where I am encouraged to be myself and discouraged from ever giving up on my dreams.

So I want you to know... that if it ever seems like there is an abundance of smiles in my eyes when I'm talking to you, they're only there because you have filled my heart so full of thanks...

for the gift of having a friend like you.

— Laurel Atherton

You're the friend who's been so good to me,
the one I tell my troubles to,
the one who listens carefully
and always understands.
You're the friend I feel closest to.
There have been so many times when
I gave you all my fears and hurts,
and each time you gave back a heart
filled with love and concern,
a shoulder to rest my worries upon,
and a tranquillity found nowhere else on earth.
You're the friend who means so much to me,
the one who feels like family in my heart.
And more than anything else,
I want you to know that I'm here for you,
just as you've always been for me...

Because you're the best friend I have.

— Barbara J. Hall

I'll Be There for You

If you've got secrets you want to tell,
we can talk all day long. If your dreams
get broken somehow, I'll remind you that
you belong. If you need someplace to
hide, you can hold my hand for a while.
If your sky begins to fall, I'll stay with
you 'til you smile. Whenever you need
some space, there's my room — you can
take it. If someone breaks your heart,
together we'll unbreak it. When you feel
sad or empty inside, I'll show you you're
not alone. If you get lost out there, I'll
come and take you home. I'll go with you
somewhere else, when you need to get
away. And when nothing seems to be
going right and you need a friend...

I'll stay.

— Ashley Rice

Our Friendship Means So Much to Me

I promise that I'll thank every wishing star that ever shined for bringing your closeness and understanding to me.

I promise that nothing will ever change the amount of appreciation I have for you. I promise that if I ever have news to share, you'll always be first on the call list. I promise — if I ever release a genie from a magic lamp — I'll share my three wishes with you. In the event that never happens, I promise that you're welcome to split any pizza I might have in my possession. (And the same goes for chocolate.)

I promise I will be there to see you through anything that tries to get you down. I promise that I'll be around through it all, I'll support you in your efforts, and I'll believe in you at all times.

And because you're such a wonderful friend, I will always feel more blessed than words will ever be able to describe. One of my hopes in life is that someday... I'll find a way to thank you for all this.

But until I do, I'll never take the beauty of our friendship for granted, and I'll never stop trying to tell you how much you mean to me.

I promise.

— L. N. Mallory

You Are a Perfect Friend

You have known me
in good and
bad times
You have seen me
when I was happy
and when I was sad
You have listened to me
when what I said was intelligent
and when I talked nonsense
You have been with me
when we had fun
and when we were miserable

You have watched me
laugh
and cry
You have understood me
when I knew what I was doing
and when I made mistakes
Thank you for
believing in me
for supporting me
and for always being ready
to share thoughts together
You are a perfect friend

— Susan Polis Schutz

The Day Our Paths Crossed, a Beautiful Friendship Began

I believe some paths are meant to cross,
to meet at friendship's door,
to share life's moments
   in togetherness, gladness,
and caring for each other.
I believe some doors are meant to be open,
to invite two people in,
to change two lives forever
   in a blessed way,
to brighten moments, filling them
   with laughter,
and to have a place that feels like home.
I believe the day we met
a special plan was designed to bring us together
so that you and I could share this life
   as the best of friends.

— Barbara J. Hall

I'm Glad We're Friends

We may not do everything together
or share every part of our lives,
but I really enjoy your company
and love spending time with you.
We have enough in common
to give us things to share and talk about,
and enough differences
to keep those talks interesting.
You often give me a new idea,
a perspective I haven't thought of,
or a delightful way of looking at something.
That's all this is for —
just to let you know
that you matter to me
and that I'm thankful for you...
and for the friendship we share.

— Barbara Cage

If there were a way to gauge what true friendship is all about...

You would get straight "A's" and pass every test with flying colors!

You are a very important and very special part of my life. I consider you to be one of the most beautiful blessings my world will ever receive. And I want you to remember, as long as you live, that there is no way I could ever get along without knowing that my
   tomorrows are going to
      have you in them.

I feel so incredibly lucky... just
   knowing that I have YOU as such a
      sweet and wonderful friend.

— R. L. Keith

A Friend Is Someone Special

A friend is someone who is concerned with everything you do • someone to call upon during good and bad times • someone who understands whatever you do • someone who tells you the truth about yourself • someone who knows what you are going through at all times • someone who does not compete with you • someone who is genuinely happy for you when things go well • someone who tries to cheer you up when things don't go well • someone who is an extension of yourself without which you are not complete •

— Susan Polis Schutz

The Depth of Friendship

"Friend."
Some people take this word for granted.
They use it to describe almost anyone
who touches their lives.
But that's not fair,
for not everyone fits this word.
It is easy to be a pal, a buddy,
a companion, or an acquaintance,
but to be a friend means so very much more...

To be a friend
means being trusted and trusting.
Honest and dedicated.
Supportive and available.
It means going strong with
your own life's work and plans,
yet reaching out to another when you're needed
(and maybe even when you're not).

To be a friend is to be fun and fair.
Serious and silly.
To make the mundane exciting.
The unexpected acceptable.
To be the silent stronghold without being asked.
To feel happy for someone else's happiness, and
to share the burden of sorrow in thought and action.

The qualifications of being a friend
are too high for the ordinary to reach.
It takes a while to earn the title
and a lifetime to truly know its meaning.
Never take the job lightly or give it away too quickly;
it must be cultivated, nurtured, and cared for.
For when you truly find a "friend,"
you are lucky enough to have one for life.

— Laura V. Nicholson

What It Means
to Be a Best Friend

A best friend is that one special person
you can lean on and laugh with,
the one you can always turn to
no matter what's going on in their world or yours.

A best friend helps you discover
a little more about yourself every day,
because they always encourage you to share
who you are and what you are feeling.

A best friend accepts you at all times.
They don't only love you <u>because</u>,
they love you <u>in spite of</u>.
They care about your happiness
as much as they care about their own.

A best friend stands beside you
when others walk away.
They never stop believing in you,
even if you stop believing in yourself.
They have the smile that hugs you,
the laughter that heals your heartaches,
and the words that always lift your spirit.

A best friend is
a one-in-a-million find,
the pot of gold at the end of the rainbow,
a treasure that gives you wealth untold.

— Vickie M. Worsham

Thank You
for Being My Friend

When things are confused
I discuss them with you
until they make sense

When something good happens
you are the first person I tell
so I can share my happiness

When I don't know what to do
    in a situation
I ask your opinion
and weigh it heavily with mine

When I am lonely
I call you
because I never feel
alone with you

When I have a problem
I ask for your help
because your wiseness helps me to solve it

When I want to have fun
I want to be with you
because we have such a great time together

When I want to talk to someone
I always talk to you
because you understand me

When I want the truth about something
I call you
because you are so honest

It is so essential
to have you in my life
Thank you for being my friend

— Susan Polis Schutz

Because We're Friends,
My Life Is So Much Happier

You have a way of saying nothing
and somehow making it feel like everything
   all at once.

I can sit beside you
and feel a comfort that no words
could possibly express.
I guess it's because
of how well you know me,
the way you finish
my sentences before I can,
or how you catch my glance across
a crowded room and know
   exactly what I'm thinking.

It's something unique inside you —
in your smile, in your eyes,
in the softest touch —
that sends a burst of confidence or
a bit of reassurance into my life.

You make the sun seem to shine brighter
and you bring happiness to the
    cloudiest of days.

Your heart is gigantic and so very caring.
I can feel it just being around you, and
that alone makes my own heart
    feel so wonderful.

You are truly amazing,
and I am truly lucky
to have you in my world.

— Vincent Arcoleo

You Have a Friend in Me

There are certain kinds of friends
who can easily discuss all things,
who feel so utterly comfortable
  with each other,
see one another's inner soul,
and keep faith when things go wrong.

For friends like these,
the length of time
they've been together
  is unimportant in determining
    how well they
       know one another,
and distance means nothing,
  for true friendship has
     no boundaries.

If we should ever grow apart
in time or distance —
today, tomorrow,
or in the days ahead —
our friendship will still
be embedded
in my mind,
my heart,
and my soul.
Regardless of where you are,
know that you have a friend
in me...
forever.

— M. Maxine Largman

I'll Always Be There
and I'll Always Care;
I'll Always Be Your Friend

There are a thousand things
I would like to be for you...
but one of the most important
is just being
    the someone you can talk to.

There are so many things
I would like to do for you,
and so many things I would like
to say and give and share.

But for today, I just want you to know
that I promise to be
    your friend for life.
I'll always be there,
    and I'll always care.

— A. Rogers

There is no need for
an outpouring of words
to explain oneself
to a friend
Friends understand each
other's thoughts even
before they are spoken

— Susan Polis Schutz

Knowing that you are always
here to understand and accept
me helps me get along in the
confused world. If every person
could have someone just like
you, the world would become
a peaceful garden.

— Susan Polis Schutz

We Have a Friendship like No Other...

Sometimes a person is blessed with meeting someone
Who will touch their life in a way
That no one else has.
You know it is something special
Right from the start.
Even if you have only known the person
For a short time,
The foundation of a true and lasting friendship
Has already been laid.

A true and lasting friendship
Is built on trust, openness, and understanding.
It is not selfish or demanding and doesn't
Require you to be someone that you are not.

Rather, it is a friendship
That gives unconditionally
And allows the freedom to express yourself
With no expectations to be anyone different.
It is giving, loving, and loyal
And welcomes the sharing of both
Good and bad times with each other.
It brings happiness
In thinking of the other person
And joy in the time that is spent together.

I have been blessed with
Such a special person in my life...
Someone whose friendship and companionship
I've grown to value and treasure.
Thank you for being such a rare individual;
Thank you for our very special friendship.

— Kathleen L. Biela

May These Wishes Come True for You

Because our friendship is one of the greatest blessings of my life, I want to wish you these things...

I wish you joy and satisfaction in everything you do, perfect health, and all you need to make life easier to do the things you want to do. I wish you good friends to call on when you need them, and I wish you love and happiness on this day and forevermore.

May the special memories you hold nourish you and remind you of your beautiful life. May your future be filled with positive experiences and realized dreams. May everyone you come in contact with celebrate your loving heart and indomitable spirit.

You're not just another friend to me.
You're one of a kind, unique, and special.
I appreciate your many virtues, and I want
you to know how important your friendship
is to me.

If I could package up these wishes and
make them all come true, they would
require more space than the world has to
offer and they would be too much for one
heart to hold. If I had my say, whatever
you want and need would be yours from
now on.

May all your dreams come true. May you
have exactly what you want. May every
kindness you've given to others be returned
to you and fill your heart with joy.

— Donna Fargo

As friends, we've developed
a wonderful trust between us.
We each know that the other is
always just a phone call away
and that if something is needed
we only have to ask.
I like the way our personalities
blend so neatly together
and how you can always make me smile.
It's nice to know that someone out there
understands who I am.
That's why I need you to know
that you're appreciated
and admired and respected
and honestly loved.
"Friend" is one of the most beautiful words I know...
Thank you for giving it so much meaning.

— Jennifer Kristin Ellis

A Lasting Friendship

Some people are fortunate enough
to meet someone with whom they share
a lasting friendship.
Even though they each may follow separate paths,
the special times spent together
and the people and places shared
are memories both will always have.
These friends are remembered always;
they live in the heart no matter what...
always just a thought or a phone call away,
even if the years have come between.

Every thought of you, my special friend,
holds a special kind of love...
Thank you for all the times in my life
you were such a vital part of,
and for being the unique essence
of our lasting friendship.

— Cammie Charles

Our Friendship Is a Wonderful Part of My Life

Our friendship has always been
the kind that lets us talk
and tell each other anything.
We've gathered our thoughts and feelings
and laid them at each other's doorstep.
We've shared a million memories —
some sad and many happy ones.
We've opened those special places
in the heart
where only best friends are welcome.
We've been through thick and thin together.

We've done our best to bring hope
    to each other
when it looked like all hope was gone.
We've always been open and honest
    with each other;
we've had the kind of friendship
    that most people never find.

What I'm trying to say is this:
As long as you have me
    and I have you for a friend,
life's never going to be lonely, boring,
or without someone special
    in our lives.
Our friendship means so much to me.

— Barbara J. Hall

This Is Why
You're My Friend

You're my friend, not because I chose you out of a group of other people or because you passed a "friend test" or because you said, "I would like to be your friend." No, none of these things made you my friend. Time, trials, joys, heartaches, understanding, love, and genuine concern made you my friend. You're unconditional. You always give me the benefit of the doubt, and when others might step away, you understand.

Yes, you're my friend because you know me and accept me for what I am. I love you.

— Jane Wright Roberts

Our Friendship

There are so many things
to do each day
There is so much going on in the world
of great concern
that often we do not stop and think about
what personally is really important
One of the nicest things in my life
is my friendship with you
and even if we don't have a lot of time
to spend with each other
I want you to always know
how much I appreciate you
and our friendship

— Susan Polis Schutz

ACKNOWLEDGMENTS

The following is a partial list of authors whom the publisher especially wishes to thank for permission to reprint their works.

PrimaDonna Entertainment Corp. for "May These Wishes Come True for You" and "Friends" by Donna Fargo. Copyright © 1999, 2001 by PrimaDonna Entertainment Corp. All rights reserved.

Barbara J. Hall for "The Day Our Paths Crossed...." Copyright © 2002 by Barbara J. Hall. All rights reserved.

Barbara Cage for "I'm Glad We're Friends." Copyright © 2002 by Barbara Cage. All rights reserved.

A careful effort has been made to trace the ownership of poems used in this anthology in order to obtain permission to reprint copyrighted materials and give proper credit to the copyright owners. If any error or omission has occurred, it is completely inadvertent, and we would like to make corrections in future editions provided that written notification is made to the publisher:

SPS STUDIOS, INC., P.O. Box 4549, Boulder, Colorado 80306.